Gallery Books
Editor Peter Fallon

THE MAP OF THE WORLD

Eiléan Ní Chuilleanáin

THE MAP
OF THE
WORLD

Gallery Books

The Map of the World
is first published
simultaneously in paperback
and in a clothbound edition
on 19 September 2023.

The Gallery Press
Loughcrew
Oldcastle
County Meath
Ireland

www.gallerypress.com

ISBN 978 1 91133 864 2 *paperback*
     978 1 91133 865 9 *clothbound*

A CIP catalogue record for this book
is available from the British Library.

The Map of the World receives financial assistance
from the Arts Council of Ireland.

the arts council chomhairle ealaíon | funding literature

Contents

THE MAP OF THE WORLD

The Miracles

for Siabhra Woods and Antonio Piacenza

Coming out of a country where emptied houses
lay open to the weather, sheep in the entry,
weedy graveyards, the foxes' cry at night
their only music; the bridge, the shifting planks
greased with a season's flattened leaves
as frost loosened its grasp; then on the far side
withered grass trampled, the briar hedge where ice
lingered underneath —
                              I could not have made it up:
how, in the tall church beside the wide calm river,
a short walk from the city walls, the poor
whose luck once seemed to have definitely run out
had made, from wooden spars and their own old clothes,
the image of deliverance, the moment
when the Virgin interfered just as the torturer
was ready to start work, or the rope broke,

the reprieve made it across the slippery bridge in time
even though the clock had been put forward
so it would come too late. Thronging the walls,
these puppets of misfortune, not the natural kind
like a mad bull or a robber or evil spirits — instead,
the tall tree of human revenge, dressed up
to look like justice, instantly bending its branches
loaded with mercy like fruit: look at their faces,
they can't believe it's true. But their truth holds out,
as when they manufactured it themselves,
the scenes of distress, their crash and agony changed
into carpentry and the needle's deliberate work.

It's the same rough craft that made the sod cabin
to defy the writ of eviction. The same bridge
spanning the gully. Fear, which is everywhere,

pushed back, and those truths, that were nearly told
at the wrong moment, were able to wait —
just as tonight the parent climbing the stairs
after three warnings feels the brush of her sleeve,
swallows back the word that can't be recalled if spoken,
and goes quietly down again.

Air: The Map of the World

The map had told us already what would happen to the
   peoples of the west —
long promontories hurrying them out into the salty
   ocean fields,
roads that twisted around inlets constantly promising a
   place to rest —
and yet invention does not falter,
just feel the tailor's clutch of the variously woven tweeds
ready for the scissors, the tacking, the silky lining, listen.
As the echoes are twisting into a macaronic language,
listen to the places we came from, their stories elbowing
   each other out of the way
(can you recall the dripping walls of the library, the lads
who were thought to be studying grammar to prepare
   for Maynooth?
but instead they were planning their forays across the
   plains of Argentina).

Up comes the prophecy I heard in the train making the
   slow journey
from Fishguard as far as the junction, when the big woman
   with red hair
in the green and white dress with a gold belt, and red shoes,
told us over and over, *they don't come back from America,*
they comes back from England, not America, they never
   comes back —
and along the carriage a man was playing an accordion,
the cards were slapped down on suitcases, do we not know
about those journeys now? or how the accordion's long
   note
spoke up in agreement? so that I could never have recalled
   her voice
except for that music, its delays and provisos,
                                          dividing up the time.

The Universe in 1300

I

I never fitted in that windy place —
but neither did they. A face, a runner
one instant in a frame, a body stuffed
half underground, they twisted
in search of rest like ancients in their beds,
not truly bodies though, yet their unrest
I felt in my own body, the urgent
hungover battering in my head, my lungs
complaining.
         Hunted by twisters and scooped
forward by demons resenting my gaze
as the forge steamed, I did not escape,
I was expelled. The blast knocking me sideways,
then stilled, but the walls, the stairs,
the precipices wanted me gone.

2 CIRCLE OF THE PRODIGALS

I spent the legacy they earned,
those ancestors that served their time
in the convent and the internment camp
refining the skills they'd studied
in homes of modest, anxious labour, of long hours
gazing at the accounts, bare bedrooms.

I spent it all on the followers of love not war
who knew where the keys of intoxication were buried;
they dealt in bribes, their lives, their bodies, currency.
The light of dawn saw them returning,
the jewels in their hats far beyond price.

In the middle Sunday of Lent I remember them,
they loved as well as I did, but love destroyed them.
They have left me staring long hours at the accounts.

3

Years ago, far away, in daylight
stronger than summers here,
we sat under the gazebo
and the voices began, their questions
brought out by the light, their explanations
reflecting light as glass flashes.

We sat on the day of the solar eclipse.
It grew a little dark, the birds interrupted their song,
the boy ran for a shaving glass and a sheet.
We watched the moving star so far away
in the dark depth of the house. All
but one remember it, and he will be a guide
when the darkness comes, until the birds
resume their song, as the light grows strong and plain.

A Shadow in Her Notebook

(Helen Moloney, stained-glass artist, 1926-2011)

She sent a ten-pound note to the Poor Clares
and imagined them in their brown habits, praying
for her to find an idea. That was a start.

They sent her a fish, swimming and wavering, its head
enormous in the dark water. They sent her a lion, then a star.
She drew the lines of lead that held the sun in its place,

that funnelled the light through what was once the open air.
The clouds paused on the mountain top:
a gleam of weather somewhere else, then the storm

pounding overhead before it slid off northward,
a dark prowl. The lion raised his paw,
coloured like the sun, glowing now

against a glass curtain, such a blue
it seemed a kind of night. The darkened interior
sucked in colours. Always the voice in her head

objecting: *But could it not just be clear glass?*
No. The shadow of the bell tower, the woman
dressed in brown, a shadow behind a screen:

they gathered around her clean white page, demanding
indigo glass for the narrow tight window
and oyster white, a little off-centre, for the loaf.

Just there on the border between the storm and the hush,
the fish trembled in the light from the clouded sky,
weaving like a hologram.
On her page the same tremble threw

a swimming shadow that covered the chancel floor.
Only the blind organist's daughter will ever see
how it shivers, floated safe in empty air.

Echo is Dumb

Without you beside me, echo is dumb as I ask what it means
to speak about the century of war and the climb towards
   peace;
it's not just the wasteland of years between lying open,
their sandstorms of change, their Ozymandias moments:

remember, when the noise retreated,
how in dappled light, stepping straight
our enemies appeared and, moving
out of the shade, slow and aloof,
dug in their pockets for the measure,
then stretched it twice. Claiming descent
from Andrew Marvell's day, they're reading
out of a page we barely see.

How could I write like him, at home
inside a verse as in a room
securely his by lock and key?
That isn't how verse came to me —
rather, in wounds and desolation;
if calm, the cold of separation.
If I speak hoping to be heard
it must be on a theme that's shared,
but how not fail, miming that voice
that reasoned in the midst of noise?

I may not leave the singular,
gripping the chart that's served so far.

The mountain roads, knotted and sprawled,
the twisted tree, the waterfall,
are only frames to hold the level
widening perspective of the civil —
but how to step in through the frame?

I remember, when the map led us
to La Verna, we came
climbing through the slim tree trunks
and the tailor was there, a pilgrim
where St Francis came searching for peace.
He recognized the cut of your clothes.

That forest, once, was famous for thieves;
the goddess honoured on the mountain chose
to make her home a refuge for the fugitives.

The Conversation

. . . and when I die
will I be transformed into a thought
travelling at the speed of light?
                                              — Philip Casey

The shiver travelling up the cat's backbone
when something flutters in the garden,
a shiver in water moving under thin ice —
that's the nearest thing to the live
thrill in the air that is Philip now.
It's a flutter that stops before finishing
since it needn't be entire to give
his singular greeting.
                                To reach it again, though,
you have to pause. The map is crumpled up,
East Arran Street hidden between the folds
where nobody searches now. I want a likeness
taken somewhere on his travels
in plain daylight by a journeyman's hand. I can see
the years of his life that were taken,
the years of work too, but the years
he gave away to the big conversation
afford his best presence, a voice
that speaks, that knows its right to a hearing:
'And this is how we spend our days'.

It echoes in the corridor
where they queued on plastic chairs.

A field full of words,
a field that Cadmus planted,
a voice that speaks about them all.

They have almost run out of chairs
but the doctor still sits in her dim
packed office, reaching still for forms to sign
to certify the condition has not changed,
as the traffic slows on the quays of the city.

Two Paintings by Nano Reid

I MAKESHIFT GATE NEAR WILDGOOSE LODGE

A horse hesitates on the edge of brightness.
In her work even water has boundaries
and segments, like a leaded window.
Here is a barrier, deliberately now
halting my advance, if roughly placed —

and now is a longer word than I had thought:
this is the art announcing, here is the place
now; the push and scrape of the brush at work
tell me how fast it was done, barring the way.
It shows she understood how
people must live hereabouts, the way
they dodge around the map, they force the place
into reluctant changes, as they need
the stopgap (and nobody who passes
imagines it will endure). A barricade explains
how they feel about time, not expecting
anything will last longer than a season,
and yet they hope it may serve
in a present continuous, marking a grammar
with useful divisions, ignoring the future
and the notorious inflated past.

2 LOAFERS

We could not save the painter's
leaf-thin imaginings:
the young man with an orange
stuffed in his groin — she painted
over that nude vision,
so which of the dark street corners
harbours his body now?

In which brown overcoat?
Is that him hesitating
hunched in the rainy twilight?
Or the man lying flat
on the warm grey metal roof
he's covering with dark thick tar?

The body retreats into
the scruffy quotidian,
still the pulse beating
in its dark refuge, now.

St Brigid's Well

1

When I asked the way to the well people knew what I meant,
and at last I found the place. There was a tree
with rosary beads and white paper
twisted around the branches. I watched a girl
who arrived just after me wearing pink trousers

and bright red sandals. She came in from the road, she stood
and prayed and reached out, stroking a stone, then moved
a few feet to the right and did it all again. Just there,
the path was a shortcut from the road to the houses,
people passed with their shopping, heading home,

one woman with a child. I heard her saying
to the child walking along in her school uniform,
'It's for all the little babies that passed away.'
I wrote her words down that same evening, to be sure
I had the truth. It was three in the afternoon,

Wednesday, in the month of June, that I caught her answer
to the question I didn't hear, in among the voices,
the cars on the road, the soft slap of the sandals
the silent visitor wore, the children coming from school.

2

Well, I thought, who needs apparitions?
But they came anyway, in spite of me,
rising like steam out of a dark patch on the road,
or matched with a burning smell
from a dark patch on an old door.

If I wanted a map that would just show the wells,
the culverted streams, the shortcuts, they came,
they congregated, they insisted, 'What about
the wall where the girls played one-two-three-O'Leary?'
they said. I said, 'Why do you want me to put that in?'

'Or Lovers' Walk?' they said. I gave them back their stare:
'What about the swan?' said I, 'I saw her just now in my
   search,
so close to me, through a gap in a high wall,
her head, her bending neck, white feathers of one wing?
How could she nest up there, and seem at ease?'

but when I turned to leave the dead end behind
and come down again beside the factory wall,
I heard the mill stream splashing downhill,
inside its prison pipe, out of the brimming pond
that I had not seen. Could I have forgotten

the excess of water, the excess of all the stories
I might have heard, as I searched for St Brigid's well?

Muriel Gifford After Her Fever

Fluttering coiling a strand of hair a phrase,
a tune remembered, not named —
is it called *fever*? the weariness
that comes after fever, even too weak to brush my hair?

(the mass of tangles at my neck like the leaves
blown into a corner, piled
by a feverish wind).
The long strand of memory twisted and blended

entwines around my hand holding the brush, and
the story my grandmother knew
catches, my mother told me she gave her
the way to untwist the long tangled locks of hair.

In those days they cut your hair off if you'd had a fever,
but Muriel's hair was lovely,
her husband prevented them cutting,
he sat beside her and used the tip of the comb,

carefully combing all the way down, slowly
stroking every long hair free
until she could wind it again
twisted in plaits and piled up as she chose.

When I finish my hair I'm too weak to begin the day
putting on your heavy carved ring,
with its dark green stone, and my mother's ring
on the other finger. My hand feels light, something swept
away, as they were swept
by the firing squad and the stifling, coiling wave.

Where Truth Lives

Settled in their orbits
the distances determined,
dependent on each other —
the bodies keep their measure.
This is where truth lives

in one material form
as with the old machines
partly still visible though
no longer in daily use —
they do not intend to change.

This is where the past lives,
the frescoes peeled away,
the portrait sold for cash
to appease a thirsty lover,

the separated bodies, the space debris
(because they move in orbit and catch
light from each other, the glance in a crowd
a crooked reflection, that glazed curve
where light flashes elated, speaking
the many forms of connection)

they enter our shared space, alongside
the word spoken to the empty passenger seat,
the gleam from the pantry, provisions for the day
    just dawning.

The Ash-tree at My Window

As in a landlord's dream the houses
change their shapes according to the season,
they bulge, then they shrink.

For five years nobody lives beside me,
my bones are bare, my spine is a tree stem
threatened with dieback.

My room on the top floor is a green cage,
Spring is here and the ash-tree is flowing
up to the window,

as a tall cloud wandering may drift
upwards a little, and closer, and
probe a tidal edge.

No need to make sense. It is there,
it whistles and tumbles. Think of a cloud,
we could not live there,

but engaging with air and element
it offers the terrace a space while it grows —
a cat on patrol.

The bare ideogram announcing *Tree*
changes annually to a flourish
of intimate leaves,

their tips barely moving, their pale approach
floating up from shady depths. Please,
hide me in summer.

Seasons of the Lemon House

The shadows in the lemon house hinted
a place of refuge, their semitones of light
carefully inclining along the downward curve,
pausing on a twilit verge. The high, dim glazed
frames gently allowing the light inside.

In the Shrovetide frost they kept their counsel.
Now on the edge where climates shift
spilling across the map, the lemon trees are safe,
herding together, brushing twigs and leaves,
the fruits floating under the ruffled skirts

shining yellow as ever. The heavy pots of clay
readied for the move outside are not yet stirring
at their slow procession. Their wheels complaining.

I thought of the nets of language, how
they float past each other: never engaging,
they lie side by side, a shallow tidal zone between.
Codes of work and home: one basks
and the other shivers — light, then dark.

The order is not spoken yet, the knife still
in the sailor's pocket. Then *cut it* —
                                  The knitted flesh
tight inside, segmented like the compass rose.

By July we will have forgotten the word for frost.

Instructions to an Architect

Rotta è l'alta colonna

1

Yours is the art that conveys
what the world is made of, where its weight
presses, and you can disguise, leading
the eye aside with colonnades —

Could you build me a shelter, showing
how a roof is carried aloft, its poise
lifted on the heads of maidens
or crouching Moors, whatever
comes handiest; and then make sure
that high window frames a chosen scene,
a tall distant pillar, as straight a figure
as I can find for courage
matched with generosity and wit,
suddenly split, fractured from the inside?

2

The child knew her bunk was all the space she needed,
her quilt a cave, her map of freedom.
She wanted everything to be fair but then she saw
the purple jar she really loved, and she pleaded —

quarrels and thunder smashing my model village,
I didn't know which of my tenants to save,
the stuffed cat or the painted wooden grandad
fallen out of his rocking chair.

3

In a closed room of giants I saw a tense fellow
who from the start needed more space, yet
pushed up his burden of stacked storeys
and only slowly forced to his knees
was crushed at last, while over ages
the old boss gods looked to carry with ease
their lighter load.   Could you make it plainer?
Next time I must try, if there is another time.

A Game

She pointed me to the house where
a child, viewed through a window in dim light,
was hopping on one foot between
the clay pots on the floor. The game was,
not to touch them with her apron
or the hem of her flying skirt.
She hopped with confidence and care,
a practised skill, and when the music
stopped, she turned and smiled.

In the garden, the solitary bee crawled out of her lair.

In Ostia, August 2020

My first night in Italy since the whole world changed —
and what has changed? The taxi driver overcharges,
he drives me past the ruins of the port and the Papal tower
to the hotel where they remember me
but also, as before, think I am German —
because of my hair? Because I am old and travelling alone?
There is food, and a glass, and I am alone
on the warm terrace looking out
on the small pool and the sunset. As before,
a cat appears exactly as the sun goes down,
and a kind of mechanical crab
with a long flex that arches like a snake swimming
begins to crawl around the bottom of the pool,
bangs its nose off the tiles, recoils and begins again.

Achilles and Phoenix

for Cormac Ó Cuilleanáin

1

I dreamed three nights about files,
about sliding drawers and labels;
as dreams declare their interest
I was dreaming a code and its keys:

just as the arrows pointed
I dreamed a token for the uncle —
the one who has to take charge
when a generation is plucked away —

the clue was a small, quite new,
quite heavy, shiny black tool
designed for a particular task
but here employed as a paperweight
keeping a stack of mismatched files
in place, held steady and together.

2

Understanding flows like the river
that slid under the house where we stayed in France,
keeping the cheeses cool in the cellar;
it flows on still to the weir, it reflects the sky
as the dream is contrived to hold in view
history's patched lining, the sewing:

an old nun writes to her niece once a fortnight;
smart Miss Healy from the shoe shop
opens the bottle of cod liver oil
to physic her widowed brother's two small sons;

a young man whose parentage
nobody asks about calls to the lawyer's office
collecting his allowance. And so on,
all the way back to the *Iliad* —

when Achilles would not listen
to the visiting Greeks, he threw them out,
except, he said, Phoenix can stay,
when I was a child he treated me kindly;
and Phoenix, who was an exile
and under a curse but found a refuge
in the house of Peleus, Achilles' father,
wept and called him his dear child,
remembering the little boy who sat on his knee at the feast,
and how afterwards Peleus asked him
to go with Achilles to Troy,
because Achilles was ignorant of the evils of war.

Milton Hears Mozart on the Mountain

He holds on fast to the guidebook. The guide has left him,
having other business. It was too dark to see.
He has evaded the devil Salmasius
and climbed warily up on the corpse of Cromwell
to emerge in a greying dawn. If he expects
that light so long withheld, effulgent, mild —
Not yet. A mountainous cold, and he shivers:
could their fiction of Purgatory be real enough
to cast a real shadow? Bodies lie here,
laid flat as autumn leaves, the slain of Drogheda,
but stir now, and pronounce their penetrating
syllabic metres. *Colkitto or Galasp?*

Liber scriptus proferetur, a voice intones.
Quintilian retches. *Can nobody here
speak decent Latin? Would a Sibyl say that?*

Ignoring him they rise with pain, and step
forward now slowly, doubtfully, as sheep
hesitate when gates open. Ariosto's
chaotic planet of loss, Astolfo's ride,
enlighten him. Mysteries of time reversed,
the dark beyond the world, revealed, now
he smells his way upward.
                                          A long way off,
a stream is venturing a brisk melody.
He imagines it serpentine, trickling
in between pebbles, making them glitter.
The stones are heavy like words, but the swift note
caressing melts them, they seem transparent,
and then the choral moment strikes: *Listen,*
the body's eye still blinded, light is flowing
into his waking dream:
                                   Lacrimosa,

but these are the tears of pleasure, and now
the angelic waitress pleads questions of love.

Sirens: with Leopold Bloom

Nothing can be compared to anything else —
was that a shadow, the shadow of a bird —
the notes dissolved in air as if it were water,

and yes, it has happened again, proportion gone,
perspective abolished. Those vibrating walls . . .
and within he waits for the shock to dissipate

slowly, as the room allows the present quarter
its share of time to pass.
                          Down there in the cellar,
confirming the worst, the cat lands on the keyboard

hitting all the barreltone base notes together.
Silence, and then she deftly trots all the way
along the white keys, only to pause where

the single high note expected to finish, so,
she waits for him; he reaches out his hand,
nailing the chord —
                          the one surviving law.

Let Me Explain

They had taken my fiddle away from me in the passage;
they said, You won't need this for a while.
When I insisted they put it away, carefully,
and brought me in, to the kitchen, to the heat —

but I knew I needed to get out of that room:
the man with his shirt open leered at my aunt
breastfeeding, and the boy was there too,
I'd been found with him before.
His brother smoked at the fireside, below
the dangling laundry. A goose on the table
half-butchered, a small naked dog under a chair —

the ladder just next to the stove
had been taken away so I tried the other door
and it led me to the flat roof beside a bedroom window.
I swear I never even looked in, I tried
the fire escape, ending on a stone terrace,

and when I shouted I could hear the words came
in a strange language and said things I knew were false.
I kept on, because I knew their conversation
was not about what was really on their minds,
how their lives would be if I could not be managed —

and what, they probably said, did I really need?
I kept on calling, afraid that if I stopped for breath —
out of breath — I would lose the power of speech for ever.

The Well

It's her mind that slides down into the darkness
(he has made a ladder out of her bones,
he treads the knuckles). Cool forests of weed
fold her in a loose embrace, keeping her
whole. She wonders, what comes next? And,
when the ladder buckles, how she knew
there was no other, this was the only way?

Still, when she comes whizzing up
again, every hair plaited, her shoes
and her stockings dry, the crease in her apron
sharp as ever, it's only the hand she keeps
hiding the bent little finger in her pocket
makes the difference between her and the two sisters
who never slid or sank or swam below —

as she did, under there, counting the stations,
the chapels, halls, the long wards. She remembers
their donor names. It's too late now to explain,
and the reason has to stay rolled up, tight
as her fist, clenched when the three sisters wait
in the locked room for him, trying his hand,
reaching in the dark, to recognize

the youngest one, with the broken little finger.

Marking the Place

1

A snug of reflections: this
hinged glass returns a clear light
off-centre, leading away
down a corridor of time.

No one in here, a flicker
catching the intruder's eye
flashes from a top window,
from the bus passing outside.

The deep glass answering back
reproves with its clear strain
whatever is half-mounted,
the rushed vice of poverty:

here is a space that is yours
for a time, judged and recalled.

2

I looked for a slip of paper to keep
the page I reached, but I touched only
the bandage I had ripped
away from my skin, where
the needle dug in, with one bloody drop.
It will do to mark the place.

A Colophon

The printer stands upright and stretches his shoulders.
The copy in all its length has been rolled up,
then pushed aside. Now comes the gathering and binding
and the journey to populate shelves alongside its peers.

This happens slowly, unlike the crowding
of bees in a swarm, but it's the same rush
to be packed together, as votes in their urn, as choirs —
the libraries, dumb in their long closed weekends, are always
attracting paper, plucked from the private office,
uprooted from barrows, into the summed catalogues.

Now the hand embraces the long expected volume,
in the clutch of paper the finger holding its place:
the margins defaced, the manicule and the asterisk land
like wasps. Released from its clasp, the book relaxes.

Home

Somebody has a perfect garden, stretching
gently uphill to a high stone wall.
Where the box hedge finishes, near the basement windows,
the grass is closely mown. The daisies
have shut up for the night. A servant girl appears —
it should be time for her dinner, but
she waits outside as the light fades, watching
the light in a first-floor window. When it goes out
she sighs and heads back indoors.
                              In the big study
a man stares at a letter written
in a language he can't understand, although
he knows the script is archaic.
He wonders again, would it be safe
to ask the schoolmaster what it all means,
although he guesses well enough
what the writer intended him to know.

For the Record

'The strangest thing was,' she said, 'I never saw
the wave. I heard his voice, just before
the boat swung. *Hold on now*. His wife grabbed a rail,
but I flew across the small cabin, the child
held so fast in my arms it seemed
I knew nothing else. We collided and then
regained our stance, there was a groan from the boat.'

'I was there,' she continued, 'and it was true.
And does it matter now? If it was real then
it matters now, even after the silence of years.'

— Since she knew the voice was the same one heard long
   before,
when she flew out of the known world, loosed
from all surroundings into a blinding truth
landed beside her, gasping like a freak wave,
groaning like a boat, and afterwards a long stillness.

1990

I heard about the man who left his family,
in a frightened call from Dublin, when I was in London
   waiting
for the first day of an absence nothing could fill.

I sat in Palmers Green in the empty front room
and I could not move to go back to the others.
(Every armchair and glass and bottle was holding still.)

But after a while I was able to move again
back to the catastrophe as it drew much nearer,
the loss no quantity of love could oppose;

and I was silent about the ones deserted, who just then
were beginning their long wait in another city, so long
that after the decades they have still found no news.

I went back to the kitchen, the receiver in one hand,
nothing in the other. Why should I try for balance?

Cat sa Leaba

Cat carad, agus mé ar cuairt chuige,
bhuail sí isteach sa seomra
nuair a bhíos chun dul a chodladh
agus ligeas di fanacht in aice liom —
bhí teas agus fionnadh uaim;
ach dúisíodh mé ag a trí a chlog,
mar bhí sí ag cíoradh mo ghruaige lena hingne
is ag brú orm, a srón beagnach sáite
isteach im' chluas. Níor dhein sí crónán ar bith,
lean uirthi ag obair chun rud éigin a chur
i gcuimhne dom, ag obair i ndáiríre
chun go dtuigfinn, ach theip uirthi,
bhí an codladh ró-throm. Ansan thosnaigh sí ag caoineadh
agus bhí orm éirí agus í a scaoileadh amach
faoin oíche, mé cosnochta ar urlár fuar.
                                        Ar maidin,
bhí ionadh orm faoin rud a tharla, ach
cén fáth nár thuigeas pé rud a bhí i gceist?
Nach mar sin a bhíonn an scéal,
an fhilíocht ag breith orainn le greim —
le greim an uafáis, sa dorchadas
is ag imeacht arís gan fiú focal amháin,
agus an dualgas fágtha aici romhainn,
an eachtra a thuiscint, conas a tharla
tiomnú cait a bheith chomh deacair san a mhíniú?

Loquitur Caliban

Ná bíodh faitíos oraibh. Tá an t-oileán plódaithe
le fuaimeanna, portaireachta binne, aoibhneas gan dochar.

Uaireanta, bíonn cling ceolmhar na mílte n-ionstraim
im' thimpeall ag crónán, is arís bhíodh glórtha,
is go fiú mé bheith múscailte tar éis bheith i mo luí le fada
chuirfeadh ar ais chun suain mé; is ansan chonac in aisling
na néalta ag oscailt chun saibhreas a nochtadh,
réidh chun titim orm, agus nuair a dhúisigh mé
thosnaigh mé ag caoineadh le fonn filleadh ar an aisling.

An Bord

le Ileana Mălăncioiu

Bhíodar ina suí ag an mbord céanna,
agus tusa sínte air, le trí lá,
ocras ortha níos measa ná riamh,
ach ní raibh fonn ar éinne
lámh a leagadh ort, ná an fheoil
bhlasta, chumhra a bhriseadh.

Thosnaíodar leis an anam,
is mar sin is gnáth arsa mise liom féin
agus mé ag féachaint tamall ortsa,
tamall eile ar na béil ar leathadh
chun na dí naofa a ól
agus cúr ag teacht uirthi

an uair inar slogadh siar í
ag an mbord céanna
gan aon eagla
is gan aon dochar a shamhlú;
Glacaidh, ithidh, do dhúisigh mé
ag béiceadh, is é seo a corpsa.

The Lad of the Skins

after Lady Gregory

So she sat there reading all the way down the page
until she came to the line where the man says,
about his own wife, speaking to the other man,
watch her all day, and when she is combing her hair
ask her then, because she is obliged, whatever
she's asked when she's combing her hair, she must agree.

The reader stopped there, the page open, her finger
marking the line, thinking of the woman
trapped, a comb in her hand. After the day,
a quarter of an hour to sit and attend to her hair,
and he comes pestering her with his questions.
And all because of the secret she knows —

about that other world, land under water,
so familiar to her, so hard for him to believe.
The reader sees her, the long hair blinding
her dark eye.
         She retreats under her hair,
as if to her lost palace under the wave.
He hears only the whistling of eels in the sea.

'Some lads were walking home late after a dance'

Although I don't know just what happened then,
the words are a warning, gripping me, alerted
as if by the sharpening breeze they felt when,
reaching the crest of the low hill,
they had a few miles yet to go,
the odd sound from far off, the cooling air
freshening their wits. The rhythm of walking,
the company, made the way seem short enough.
A shadow, hare or cat, was crossing the road
where it sloped gently downward from the cross.

And what was shown to them there,
what words were spoken? Although
(since this is a typical episode)
I can guess, an encounter, a door
opening to an urgent world,
which needs to speak, which asks for help.
One of them was called by his name
and given a message to pass on
to a neighbour of his own.
All three saw, four fields away,
a light in the ruined house.
The story is current still in the place.
They never forget that meeting,
but remember especially how wide awake,
how ready they had felt, at midnight
outside the dancehall, calling out goodbye
before turning together for the road home.

The Bishop and His Sisters

The question was too hard for them, so they went and
  asked the Bishop.

After they left he turned in his chair
and took down the big book from Salamanca.
He opened at the page, and read,
'A woman naturally beautiful, dressed
in the usual fashion of her native country,
is allowed to walk along a certain street
even if she knows that somebody there
will commit sin when he sees her. Occasionally,
she might go around the longer way,
if not very inconvenient.'
               He closed the book,
and thought about her stepping on the cobbles
between the grooms and the horses, if she tried
going round by the long lane beside the stables.
A woman naturally beautiful. How long
since he looked straight in a woman's face? He remembered
his own sisters, how he'd see the three of them
filling big jugs together at the pump
so they could wash themselves, and the soft knock
to be heard from their bedroom, and sometimes a splash,
and how they looked when they came downstairs,
their hair in plaits, their faces fresh and calm,
able to face the day, and the day's work.

Noah's Ark

after Ileana Mălăncioiu

Fear is spreading like a weed,
spreading like fire in a meadow,
it spreads like water over the whole earth
and Noah's ark is still not finished.

When there are no timbers, no pitch,
when seven pairs of beasts cannot be found,
when Noah's sons are not at home,
when Noah is not in the best of shape.

I saw him yesterday shaking all over,
he's stiffened like an old suit of armour,
and he stares at the muddy waters
which nobody is going to escape.

It was not I who decided, he seems to say
staring everywhere at once
like a wild thing cornered, even though for ages
all around him there has been nothing but the flood.

What Happened Next?

So, will we ever be told what happened afterwards
to the man who had fallen among thieves
as he went down from Jerusalem to Jericho:
half killed, what happened to him
after the Samaritan paid for his care at the inn?

Or what became of the women in Naples in 1944
who sold rough sex to soldiers in public for food,
their faces never changing as they took it?
How can I even ask, who would I ask? Indeed,
it was never the point of the story.

Fiction or truth, it will be told again:
This happened in my lifetime in a place that I know —
the moment the light falls on the victim and then
it moves away slowly, the light
that also falls when there's nobody there to see it.

When I begin the telling the words will not be quiet,
I have to lie down beside them and listen
to the crackling syllables that keep beginning again
each time the wheel of language spins,

but they never tell what happened after the ending.
They have so many stories, and not all
have been heard already, and not all of them
can tell us clearly what we ought to have done.

War Time

The convent now is full of women down on their luck,
abandoned wives, mothers in law,
nieces and daughters of men who needed
to vanish for a while. Avoiding each other,
waiting, reading a little or sometimes
wasting an hour drafting a letter —
they slip upstairs to dig in backpacks, hunting
for the last envelope with a real address.

Where do they all sleep? The young ones camp
in the refectory, under the frescoed arch.
The girl who finished in boarding school has nowhere to go
now, her home is beyond the new border.
She practises scales on the tablecloth, breathing
in four-four time. Then she begins the concerto,
first with a gallop, then a long pause
counting the bars, her fingers held up in the air.

It is time. The women have drifted singly down
along the short path leading to the chapel,
the sisters' voices heard, as the door opens,
a brief crescendo. At the edge of the table
she waits until a sign from her dead music mistress
tells her to bring the spread fingers down.
She holds the chord in place pressing her foot
into the floor, the note sinking into time,

the time that's lost, the note so much older
than the hand that conjures, filling the empty room.

2021

Acknowledgements and Notes

Acknowledgements are due to the following publications where some of these poems, or versions of them, were published first: *Cyphers, The Irish Times, Poetry Ireland Review* and *Poetry London*.

Thanks also are due to the Tyrone Guthrie Centre at Annaghmakerrig.

'The Miracles' was commissioned for a film, *Hunger's Way* by Edwina Guckian and Vincent Woods. Strokestown International Poetry Festival, 2021.

'Air: The Map of the World' was written for a volume in memory of Mícheál Ó Súilleabháin.

'The Universe in 1300' was written for *Divining Dante* on the 700th anniversary of Dante's death (Recent Work Press, 2021).

'A Shadow in Her Notebook' appeared in *ABEI Journal: The Brazilian Journal of Irish Studies* special issue in memory of Eavan Boland, 2021.

'Echo is Dumb' appeared in *Companions of His Thoughts More Green* edited by David Wheatley (Broken Sleep Books, 2022), a volume commemorating the 400th anniversary of the birth of Andrew Marvell.

'The Conversation' was written for a volume in memory of Philip Casey.

'St Brigid's Well' appeared in an exhibition catalogue, St Brigid's Day 2022, Hamilton Gallery, Sligo.

'Muriel Gifford After Her Fever' was written for *Eamon at 80,* a festschrift published by The Gallery Press, 2022.

'Seasons of the Lemon House' was written for an online exhibition of photographs by students at the Siena Art Institute.

'In Ostia, August 2020' appeared in *Days of Clear Light*, for Jessie Lendennie, 2021.

'Achilles and Phoenix' and 'A Colophon' were published in *Liber Amicorum* for Cormac Ó Cuilleanáin, Trauben, 2022.

'Sirens: with Leopold Bloom' was written for the programme of the International Joyce Symposium, Dublin, 2022.

'Milton Hears Mozart on the Mountain' was written for a meeting of the Milton Society of America, April, 2022.

'Loquitur Caliban' was translated from *The Tempest* for the celebration of the 400th anniversary of the first folio of Shakespeare's plays at Trinity College Dublin, 2023.